AL•LEONARD
ro vocal®
BETTER THAN KARAOKE!

WOMEN'S EDITION
VOLUME 16

Disney's FAVORITES

W9-BMZ-464

Disney Characters and artwork © Disney Enterprises, Inc.

WONDERLAND MUSIC COMPANY, INC.
WALT DISNEY MUSIC COMPANY

ISBN 978-1-4234-0110-0

DISTRIBUTED BY
HAL•LEONARD® CORPORATION
7777 W. BLUEMOUND RD. P.O. BOX 13819 MILWAUKEE, WI 53213

In Australia Contact:
Hal Leonard Australia Pty. Ltd.
4 Lentara Court
Cheltenham, Victoria, 3192 Australia
Email: ausadmin@halleonard.com

For all works contained herein:
Unauthorized copying, arranging, adapting, recording, Internet posting, public performance, or other distribution of the printed or recorded music in this publication is an infringement of copyright.
Infringers are liable under the law.

Visit Hal Leonard Online at
www.halleonard.com

CONTENTS

PAGE	TITLE	DEMO TRACK	SING-ALONG TRACK
4	BIBBIDI-BOBBIDI-BOO (THE MAGIC SONG) Cinderella	1	9
6	CAN YOU FEEL THE LOVE TONIGHT The Lion King	2	10
10	A DREAM IS A WISH YOUR HEART MAKES Cinderella	3	11
14	I WON'T SAY (I'M IN LOVE) Hercules	4	12
17	IF I NEVER KNEW YOU (Love Theme from POCAHONTAS) Pocahontas	5	13
21	REFLECTION Mulan	6	14
23	A WHOLE NEW WORLD Aladdin	7	15
27	WRITTEN IN THE STARS Aida	8	16

Bibbidi-Bobbidi-Boo
(The Magic Song)

from Walt Disney's CINDERELLA

Words by Jerry Livingston
Music by Mack David and Al Hoffman

© 1948 Walt Disney Music Company
Copyright Renewed
All Rights Reserved Used by Permission

Ab Fm Bb7
men - chic - ka - boo - le - roo, but the thing - a - ma - bob that
Fm Bb7 Eb7 Bb7 Eb7 G7
does the job is bib - bi - di - bob - bi - di - boo.
Refrain
Ab Abdim7
Si - di - di - doo - doo, doo - de - li - don - da, did - di - li - did - di - li -
Ab Eb7
doo. Doo - bi - di - doo - bi - di, doo doo doo doo,
doo - de - li - doo - de - li, doo - de - li - doo - de - li, dee - de - li - doo - de - li -
Ab Bb7/Ab Eb7 Eb7sus Eb7 Ebdim7
doo!
Outro
Eb7 Ab/Eb Eb9 Bbm7 Eb7
Bib - bi - di - bob - bi - di,
Bbm7 Eb7 Bbm7 Eb7 Ab
bib - bi - di - bob - bi - di, bib - bi - di - bob - bi - di - boo.

Can You Feel The Love Tonight

from Walt Disney Pictures' THE LION KING

Music by Elton John
Lyrics by Tim Rice

© 1994 Wonderland Music Company, Inc.
All Rights Reserved Used by Permission

Chorus
D A/C♯ Bm G D G E/G♯
can you feel the love to - night? It is where we are.
A G D/F♯
It's e - nough for this
Bm D/A G Em7 D/F♯ G6 E/G♯
wide - eyed wan - der - er that we got this far.
A D A/C♯ Bm G
And can you feel the love to - night,
D G E/G♯ A
how it's laid to rest?
G D/F♯ Bm D/A G
It's e - nough to make kings and vag - a - bonds be -
Em7 D/F♯ G6 A G/D D
lieve the ver - y best.

Interlude
D A/C♯ G/B D/F♯ G D/F♯ A/C♯ D Em7 D/F♯
Verse
G D/F♯ G D/F♯
There's a time for ev-'ry-one, if they on-ly learn
G D/F♯ Em7 A
that the twist-in' ka-lei-do-scope moves us all in turn.
G D/F♯ G D/F♯
There's a rhyme and rea-son to the wild out-doors
G Bm7 C
when the heart of this star-crossed voy-a-ger beats in time with yours.
Chorus
A D A/C♯ Bm G
And can you feel the love to-night?
D G E/G♯ A G D/F♯
It is where we are. It's e-nough for this

Bm D/A G Em7 D/F♯ G6 E/G♯
wide - eyed wan - der - er that we got this far.
A D A/C♯ Bm G
And can you feel the love to - night,
D G E/G♯ A
how it's laid to rest?
G D/F♯ Bm D/A G
It's e - nough to make kings and vag - a - bonds be -
Em7 D/F♯ G6 A G/D D
lieve the ver - y best.
Outro
G D/F♯ Bm D/A G
It's e - nough to make kings and vag - a - bonds be -
Em7 D/F♯ G6 A G/D D
lieve the ver - y best.

A Dream Is A Wish Your Heart Makes

from Walt Disney's CINDERELLA

Words and Music by Mack David, Al Hoffman and Jerry Livingston
(with additional music and lyrics by David Pack)

© 1948 Walt Disney Music Company
This arrangement © 1995 Walt Disney Music Company and Wonderland Music Company, Inc.
Copyright Renewed
All Rights Reserved Used by Permission

Emaj9 C(♭5) D/E E13♭9 B♭7
some - day your rain - bow will come smil - in'
Amaj9 A6 Amaj7 D9♯11 D7
through. No mat - ter how your heart is griev - ing, if
Eadd9 C♯m11 F♯ F♯m7 A/B B13♭9
you keep on be - liev - ing, the dream that you wish will come
Eadd9 F♯m7/B Emaj9 G7/B Am7/B F♯m7 F♯m7/B
true.
Verse
Eadd9 B13♭9/E Emaj9 C(♭5)/E
A dream is a wish your heart makes
Eadd9 G♯7 Aadd9 G♯m7 C♯7♭9
when you're feel - in' small. A -
F♯madd9 F♯m(♯5) F♯m6 F♯m7
lone in the night you whis - per, think - in'
A/B B7 Emaj9 C(♭5) F♯m7/B
no one can hear you at all. You

Eadd9 B13♭9/E Emaj9 A/B
wake with the morn - ing sun - light to find
Bm7 E13 E7♭13 Amaj9 A6
for - tune that is smil - in' on you. Don't let your
Amaj7 D9♯11 D7 Am/E E C♯m11 F♯9
heart be filled with sor - row. For all you know, to - mor - row the
F♯m7 A/B B13♭9 Eadd9 F♯m7/B Emaj9 F♯m7/B
dream that you wish will come true.
Interlude
Gmaj9 Cmaj7 Gmaj9 Fmaj9 Emaj9 F♯m7/B Emaj9 F♯m7/B
Verse w/Instrumental
Gmaj9 G13 Cmaj7/G Gm7 C7 Fadd9 C13♭9/F
A dream is a wish your
Fmaj9 E/F Fadd9 A7♯5 B♭add9 Am11 D7
heart makes. A
Gmadd9 Gm(♯5) Gm6 Gm7 B♭maj7/C C7♭9
dream is a wish your heart makes.

Fmaj9 Dbmaj9 Bb/C Fadd9 C13b9/F Fmaj9 E/F F
You wake with the morn - ing sun - light to find
Cm7 F13 F7b13 Bbmaj9 Bb6
for - tune that is smil - in' on you. Don't let your
Bbmaj7 Eb9#11 Eb7 Fadd9 Dm7 G9
heart be filled with sor - row. For all you know, to - mor - row the
Gm7 Bb/C C13b9 Fadd9 A7#5
dream that you wish will come true. No mat - ter
Bbmaj9 Eb9#11
how your heart is griev - ing, if
Bbm/F F Dm7 G7 Bbadd9 Am7 Dm7 Gm7
you keep on be - liev - ing, the dream that you wish will come
Outro
Bbmaj7/C C7 Fmaj7 Gm7/C Fmaj7 Gm7/C
true.
Fmaj7 Ab13/Eb Dbadd9 Bb/C Fmaj9#11
rit.

I Won't Say
(I'm in Love)

from Walt Disney Pictures' HERCULES

Music by Alan Menken
Lyrics by David Zippel

© 1997 Wonderland Music Company, Inc. and Walt Disney Music Company
All Rights Reserved Used by Permission

Chorus
C G/C C G/B Am G/A Am
No chance, no way, I won't say it, no, no.
C/G F G/F Fmaj7/G G
It's too cli - ché. I won't say I'm in
Verse
C C/G G C
love. I thought my heart had learned its
F6 C/E
les - son. It feels so good when you start
F/G G Am C/D D7
out. My head is scream - ing, "Get a grip, girl.
G N.C. F/G G F/G G
Un - less you're dy - in' to cry your heart out."
Pre-Chorus
C F G C Am
Oh.
F C/E Dm7 G7sus G7
Whoa, oh.

Chorus
C G/C C G/B Am G/A Am
No chance, no way, I won't say it, no, no.
C/G F G/F Fmaj7
This scene won't play. I won't say I'm in
G F/G G C G/C C
love. You're way off base,
G/B Am G/A Am
I won't say it. Get off my case,
C/G F G/F Fmaj7/G G
I won't say it.
C Am
Oh.
Slowly, freely
Fmaj7 G/F Fmaj7/G G
At least out loud, I won't say I'm in
Outro
Steady, but slower
C C/G C C/G C C/G C
rit.
love.

If I Never Knew You
(Love Theme from POCAHONTAS)

from Walt Disney's POCAHONTAS

Music by Alan Menken
Lyrics by Stephen Schwartz

© 1995 Wonderland Music Company, Inc. and Walt Disney Music Company
All Rights Reserved Used by Permission

Cm7 B♭add9/D F/E♭ E♭/F
lost for - ev - er, if I nev - er knew
Bridge
F/E♭ E♭maj7 F/E♭ E♭maj7 Dm11
you. Some - how it'd make the whole world
Gm11
right. I nev - er knew that fear and
E♭maj9 B♭add9/D Gm7 Dm7
hate could be so strong, all they'd leave us were these whis - pers in the
E♭maj9 Cm11 Dm7
night. But still my heart is say - ing we were
Verse
E♭maj9 E♭/F F/G C
right. Oh. If I nev - er
Am11 Am7 C Am11 Am7
knew you, if I nev - er knew your love,

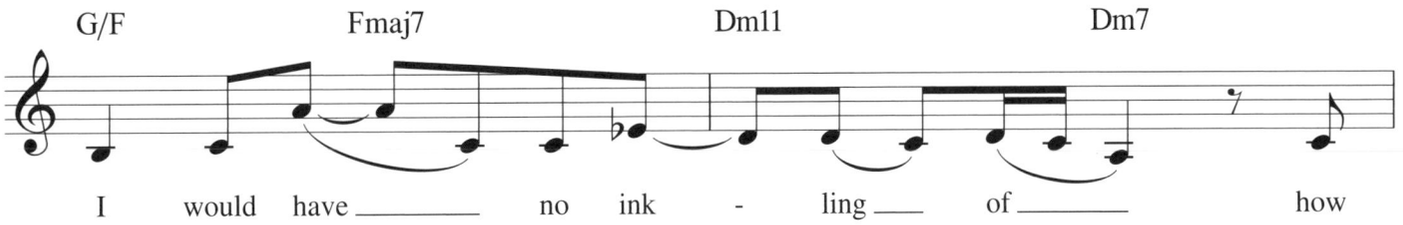
G/F
Fmaj7
Dm11
Dm7
I would have no ink - ling of how

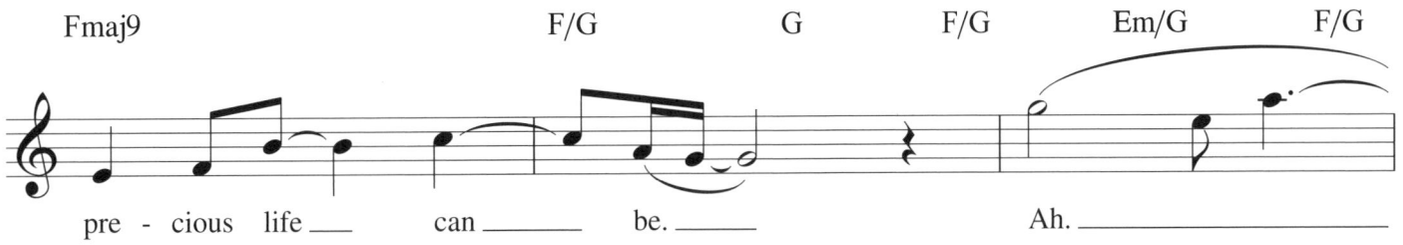
Fmaj9
F/G
G
F/G
Em/G
F/G
pre - cious life can be.
Ah.

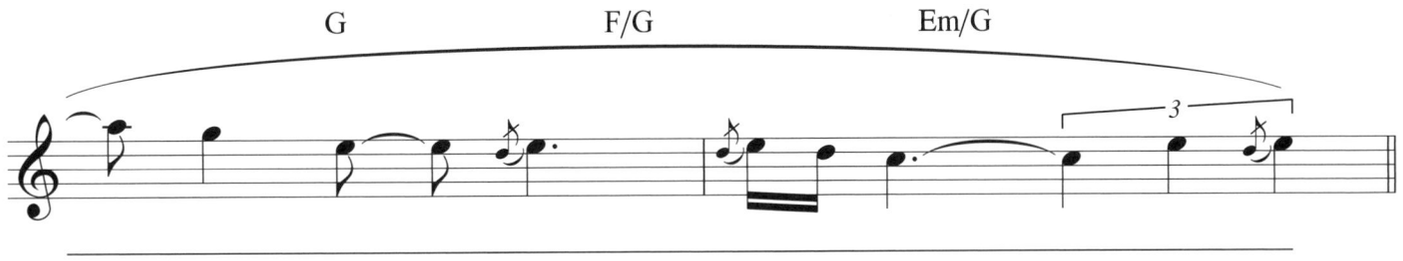
G
F/G
Em/G
3

Bridge

G/F
Fmaj7
G/F
3
I thought our love would be so beau - ti - ful,
(So beau - ti - ful.)

Em11
Some - how we'd make the whole world right.

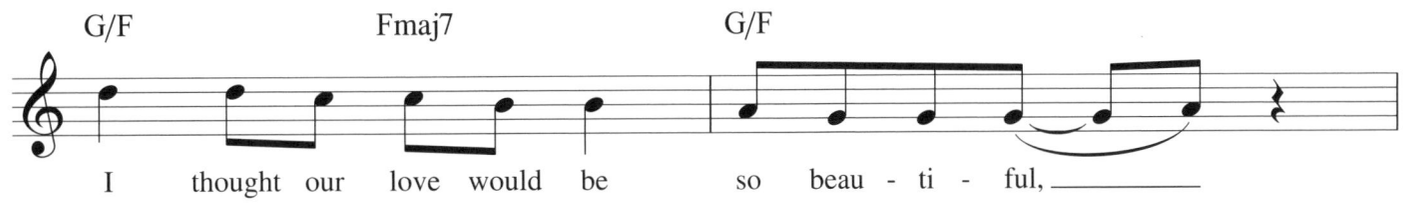
G/F
Fmaj7
G/F
I thought our love would be so beau - ti - ful,

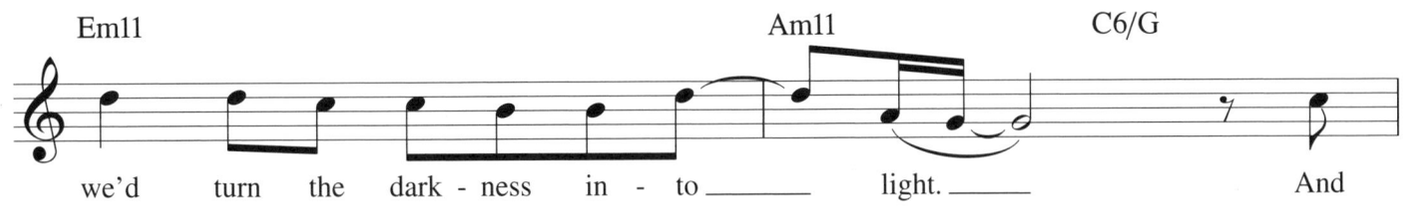
Em11
Am11
C6/G
we'd turn the dark - ness in - to light.
And

Dm11
Em7
Fmaj9
still my heart is say - ing we were right.
Verse
G♭maj7/A♭
rit.
D♭
a tempo
B♭m11
B♭m7
If I nev - er knew
A♭/D♭
Fm7
G♭maj9
E♭m7
Fm7
G♭2
E♭m7
Fm7
Emp - ty as the sky,
nev - er know - ing
G♭maj9
rit.
why.
B♭m7
a tempo
D♭maj9/F
Lost for - ev - er,
Outro
G♭maj7
rit.
if I nev - er knew
G♭/A♭
A♭
D♭
a tempo
B♭m7
you.
G♭maj9
G♭/A♭
rit.
D♭add9
Ooh.

Reflection

from Walt Disney Pictures' MULAN
Music by Matthew Wilder
Lyrics by David Zippel

© 1998 Walt Disney Music Company
All Rights Reserved Used by Permission

Chorus
A♭ E♭/F Fm7 E♭/D♭ D♭
Who is that girl I see, star - ing straight
D♭m(maj7) D♭m6 A♭ E♭/G Fm7 Cm/E♭ D♭maj7
back at me? Why is my re - flec - tion some - one
G♭add9 E♭7
I don't know? Some - how I
E♭/F Fm7 E♭/D♭ D♭ D♭m(maj7) D♭m6
3
can - not hide who I am, though I've tried.
A♭ E♭/G Fm7 Cm/E♭ D♭maj7 D♭m
When will my re - flec - tion show who I am in -
Fm Cm/E♭ Dm7♭5 A♭ E♭/G Fm7 Cm/E♭ D♭maj7
rit.
a tempo
- side? When will my re - flec - tion show
Outro
D♭m A♭ Fm7 A♭
who I am in - side?

A Whole New World

from Walt Disney's ALADDIN

Music by Alan Menken
Lyrics by Tim Rice

© 1992 Wonderland Music Company, Inc. and Walt Disney Music Company
All Rights Reserved Used by Permission

Dbadd9 Gb/Db Gbmaj7/Bb Abadd9/C
in - de - scrib - a - ble feel - ings.
Ebm6/Gb F7 Bbm Fm/Ab
Soar - ing, tum - bling, free - wheel - ing through an
Gb Db
end - less dia - mond sky. A whole new
Chorus
Ab Ab/C Db Ab Ab7/C
world, a hun - dred thou - sand things to see.
Db Ab/Gb Db/F Ab/Gb Db/F
I'm like a shoot - ing star, I've come so far. I
Bbm11 Eb7 Gb/Ab
can't go back to where I used to be.
Ab Ab/C Db Ab/C Adim7

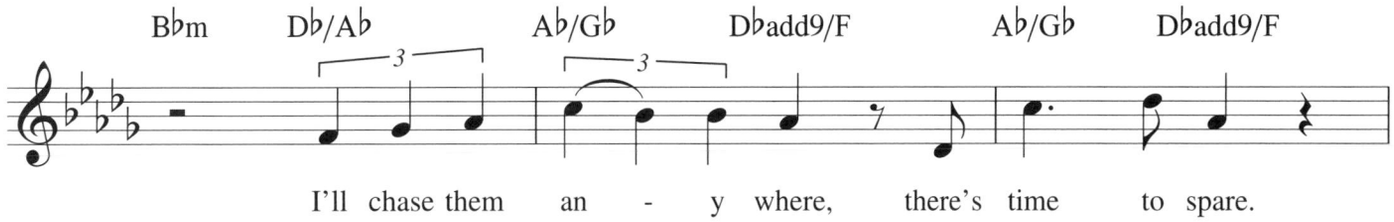
Bbm Db/Ab Ab/Gb Dbadd9/F Ab/Gb Dbadd9/F
I'll chase them an - y where, there's time to spare.

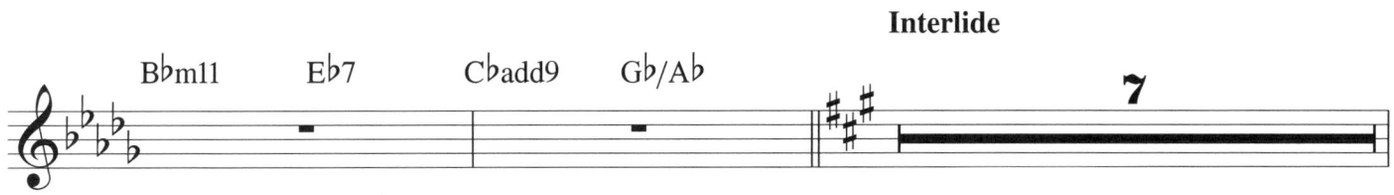
Interlide
Bbm11 Eb7 Cbadd9 Gb/Ab
7

Chorus
G/A N.C. A6/C# D
A whole new world.

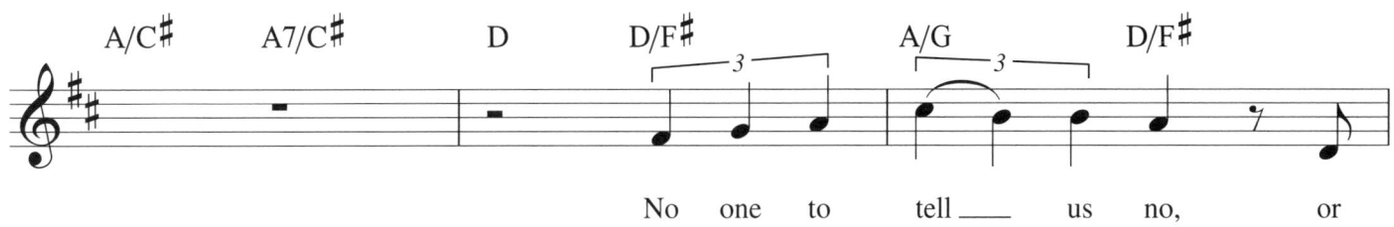
A/C# A7/C# D D/F# A/G D/F#
No one to tell us no, or

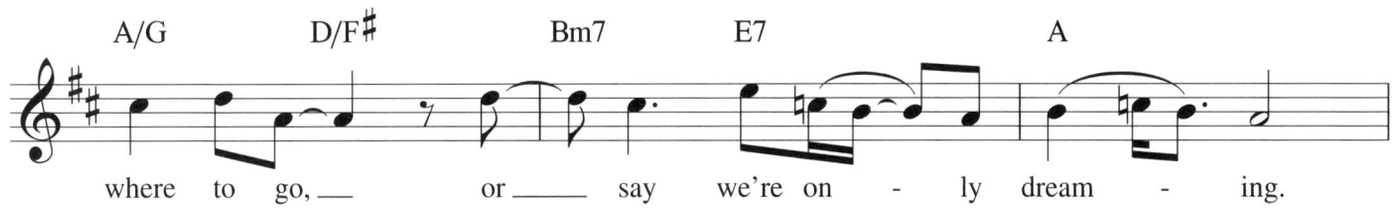
A/G D/F# Bm7 E7 A
where to go, or say we're on - ly dream - ing.

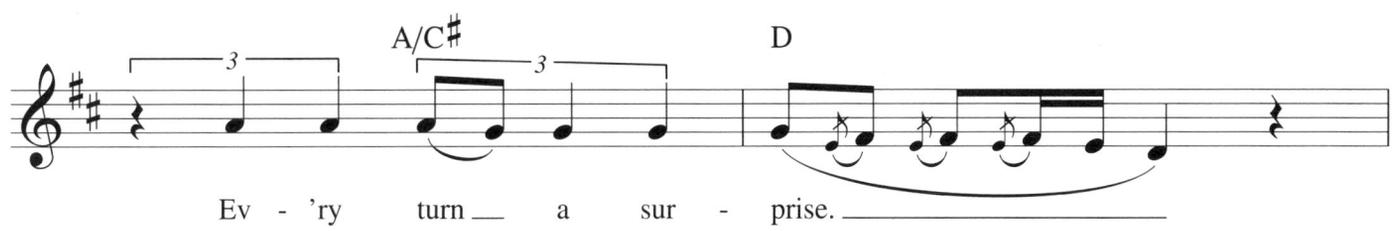
A/C# D
Ev - 'ry turn a sur - prise.

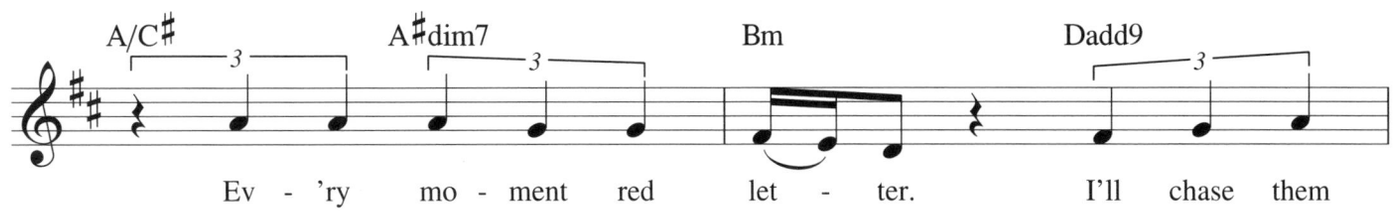
A/C# A#dim7 Bm Dadd9
Ev - 'ry mo - ment red let - ter. I'll chase them

A/G D/F♯ A/G D/F♯
an - y - where, there's time to spare.
G7♯11 F♯m7 A♯dim7 Bm E7sus E7
An - y - where. Let me share.
Cadd9 G/A Bm7 E9/G♯
rit.
Ooh.
Outro
N.C. F♯m7 D/F♯ Gadd9
a tempo
A whole new world, that's where we'll
F♯m7 D/F♯ Gadd9 F♯m7 D/F♯
be. A thrill - ing place
G/A Dadd9 G/D Dadd9
rit. a tempo
for you and me.
Dadd9 G/D Gmaj7/B A/C♯ Dadd9
rit.
Ooh, yeah.

Written in the Stars

from Elton John and Tim Rice's AIDA

Music by Elton John
Lyrics by Tim Rice

© 1999 Wonderland Music Company, Inc., Happenstance Ltd. and Evadon Ltd.
All Rights Reserved Used by Permission

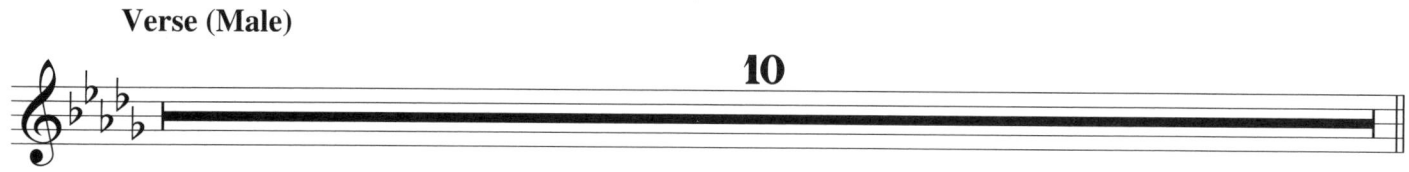

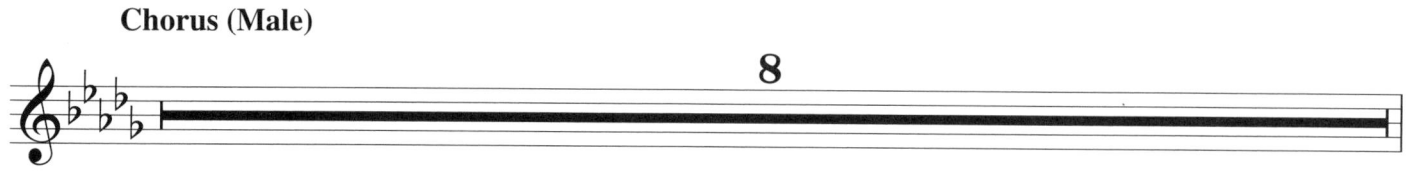

Marry the princess, Radames. You can help my people. This could be our chance to do something important.

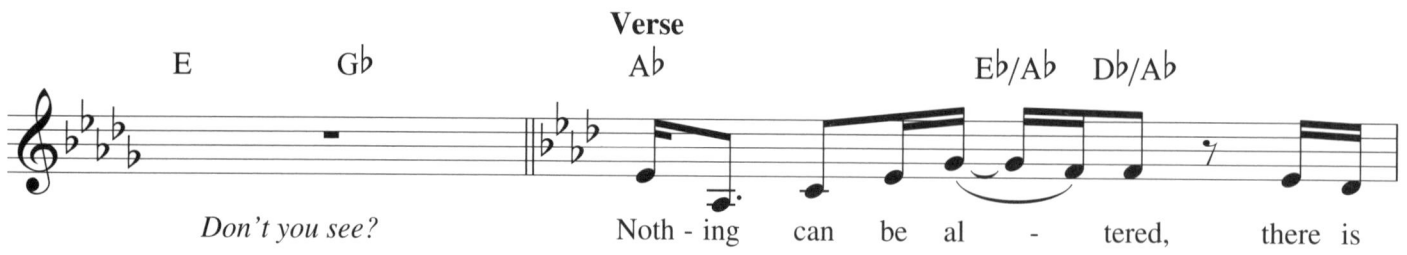

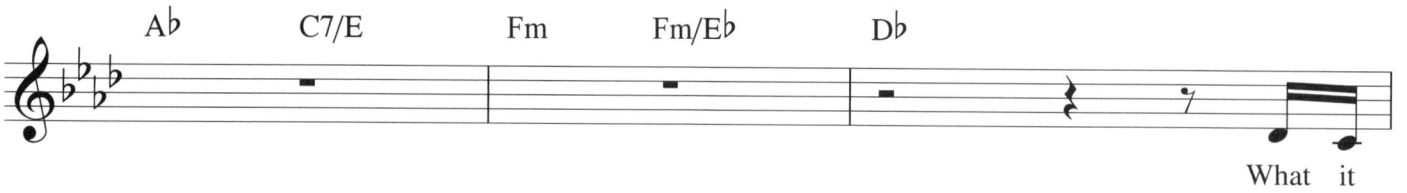

B♭m
E♭sus
E♭
is to be in love, and have that love re - turned. Is it
Chorus
D♭
B♭m
writ - ten in the stars? Are we pay - ing for some crime? Is that
G♭maj7
E♭m
G♭/A♭
all that we are good for, just some stretch of mor - tal time?
D♭
A♭/C
B♭m7
D♭/A♭
God's ex - per - i - ment, in which we have no say, in
G♭
D♭/F
E♭m
A♭7sus A♭7
which we're giv - en par - a - dise, but on - ly for a day.
Outro
D♭
A♭/D♭ G♭/D♭
D♭
A♭/D♭ G♭/D♭
A
rit.
B
D♭